SAVING OUR WORLD

OCEANS

Jane Parker

Franklin Watts
London • Sydney

© Aladdin Books Ltd 1999
New edition published in 2003
Designed and produced by
Aladdin Books Ltd
28 Percy Street
London W1T 2BZ

ISBN 0-7496-5095-8

First published in Great Britain in 1999 by
Franklin Watts
96 Leonard Street
London EC2A 4XD

Printed in UAE

Editor: Michael Flaherty
Designer: Karen Lieberman
Some of the illustrations in this book have appeared in previous titles
published by Aladdin Books.
A CIP catalogue record for this book
is available from the British Library.

The author, Jane Parker, gained her zoology degree and then went to work at
London Zoo to study the reproductive biology of rare mammals. For the last 13 years
she has been involved in writing books on wildlife and science subjects.

The consultant, Steve Parker, is a writer and editor of life sciences, health and
medicine, and has written many books for children on science and nature.

ABOUT THIS BOOK

This book is divided into chapters that lead the reader through this topic.
First we discover what and where the oceans are and why they are so
important to the environment. We learn about the inhabitants of the
oceans and how they depend on each other for survival. We see not only
the wealth of food and products that the world gets from the oceans, but
also how we are destroying this bounty. Finally, we learn of ways to
stop this destruction.

Throughout the book are stimulating **Talking Points**, outlined in the
extended contents, aimed at raising greater awareness and provoking
discussion about important environmental topics and issues. These are
further backed up at the end of the book by a **Look Back and Find**
section where questions test the reader's new-found knowledge of the
subject and encourage further thought and discussion.

Contents

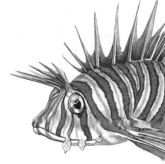

Oceans in Crisis

Unknown world

The oceans are vast – they cover almost three-quarters of the Earth's surface. Yet we know very little about them. We are only now learning about conditions in the dark depths, how the water behaves, and what creatures live there.

The water goes around in a never-ending cycle from the oceans to the clouds, then as rain to rivers, and back to the ocean. The Sun's energy drives this cycle. It also makes the ocean currents swirl around the Earth and these, in turn, affect the weather above them.

Troubled waters

People have used the oceans for thousands of years to provide food, to travel, trade and explore, to have fun, as a giant rubbish tip and, more recently, to drill for oil and gas. The oceans are so vast that no one ever thought these activities would have any effect on them. But they have and today the oceans are in trouble.

The air and water seem to be warming up, which may lead to more events like the warm Pacific Ocean current, El Niño. This has led to many drastic changes in the world's weather patterns, like a storm on the Californian coast (above).

CHAPTER ONE

What is an Ocean?

Water world

We think of our world as being solid ground, but 71% of the Earth's surface is covered by oceans. The oceans are wide and very deep in places. They contain an unimaginably huge volume of water – 1,300 million cubic km (300 million cubic miles).

World oceans

There are five great oceans (see map, right), though they are all linked together by watery channels. The largest is the Pacific Ocean which covers nearly half of the planet. The smallest is the Arctic which covers the North Pole. Lots of smaller seas bulge around the edges of the oceans.

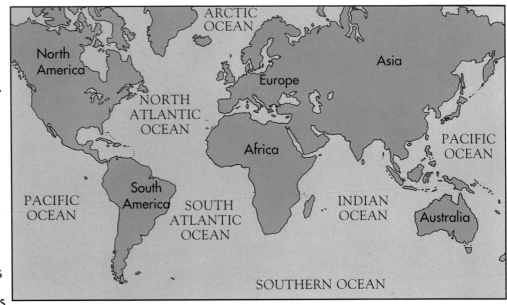

ARCTIC OCEAN

North America

Asia

Europe

NORTH ATLANTIC OCEAN

PACIFIC OCEAN

Africa

South America

PACIFIC OCEAN

SOUTH ATLANTIC OCEAN

INDIAN OCEAN

Australia

SOUTHERN OCEAN

❶ Steam and other gases from volcanoes

❷ Vapour forms clouds in the new atmosphere.

Rainfall

❸ Hollows fill with water and become the oceans.

How the oceans formed

About 4,600 million years ago, as the Earth formed, molten rocks spat out gases, such as carbon dioxide and steam (water vapour), from violent volcanic eruptions (1). These gases formed the atmosphere, the steam formed clouds, and it began to rain (2). The downpour lasted many thousands of years, and the water gradually filled the hollows in the planet's wrinkled surface to become the oceans (3).

Water cycle

Water goes around in a never-ending cycle. At the sea's surface, the Sun's heat turns water into a gas in the air called water vapour. This is evaporation. The water vapour rises into the sky where it cools and turns back to droplets of water. This is called condensation. The droplets form the clouds, and they get bigger until they become so heavy they fall back down as rain. The water runs over the land into rivers and lakes and eventually back to the sea.

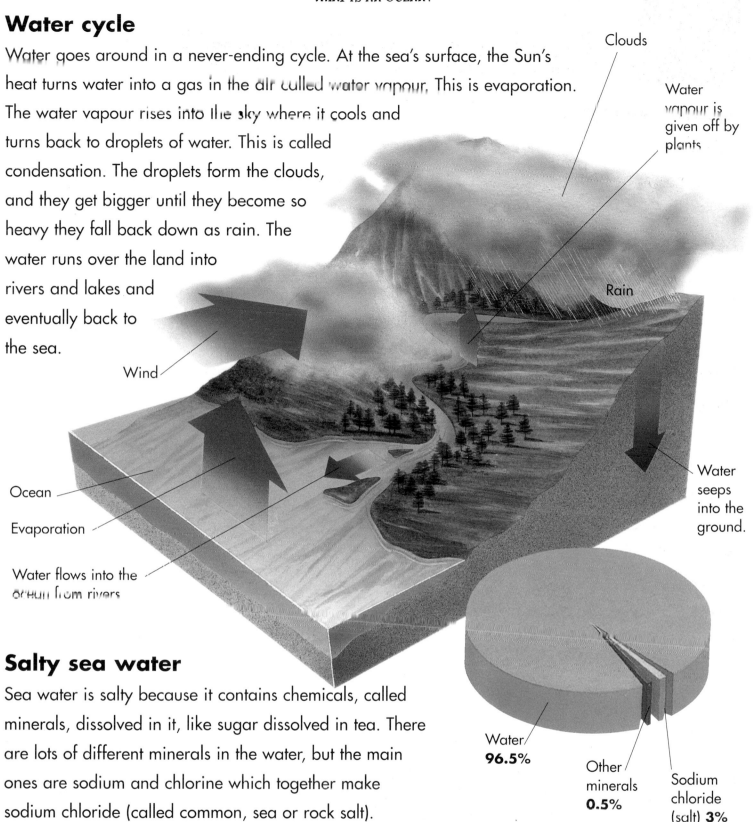

Clouds

Water vapour is given off by plants

Rain

Wind

Ocean

Evaporation

Water flows into the ocean from rivers

Water seeps into the ground.

Salty sea water

Sea water is salty because it contains chemicals, called minerals, dissolved in it, like sugar dissolved in tea. There are lots of different minerals in the water, but the main ones are sodium and chlorine which together make sodium chloride (called common, sea or rock salt).

Water **96.5%**

Other minerals **0.5%**

Sodium chloride (salt) **3%**

TALKING POINT

Most of the ocean is very deep – between 3 and 6 km (2 to 4 miles). Can you imagine how deep this is?

A: If you walk quickly for about an hour, you will cover 3 to 6 km (2 to 4 miles). Now imagine this distance going straight down into the water. As you go deeper and deeper, the pressure of the water builds up very quickly, and it becomes pitch black and near freezing.

The shape of the ocean

The ocean floor is a vast "seabed-scape" of gentle hills, steep cliffs, deep valleys, vast plains and the biggest mountains on Earth. But it is not fixed – it is always moving. It takes millions of years to move from where it is formed to where it is destroyed. The edge of the sea is called the coast, and it too is always changing as the waves and currents reshape the shore.

Ocean floor

The ocean floor is formed in deep mid-oceanic ridges (below) where molten rock bubbles up from beneath the Earth's crust. The new rock solidifies and pushes the ocean floor towards the shore. There it sinks back into the molten mantle as it is pushed under the land (continental crust).

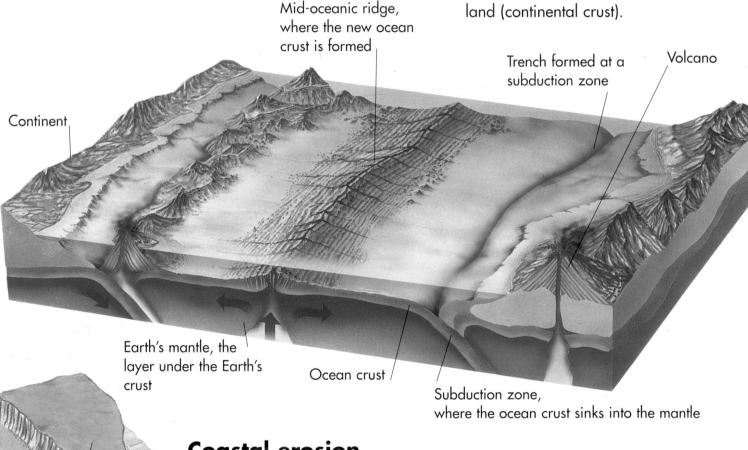

Mid-oceanic ridge, where the new ocean crust is formed

Trench formed at a subduction zone

Volcano

Continent

Earth's mantle, the layer under the Earth's crust

Ocean crust

Subduction zone, where the ocean crust sinks into the mantle

Coastal erosion

Caves

Headland

Cliffs

Arch

Stack

Along the coast, the waves pound the shore, hurling pebbles and sand that chip away at the cliffs. This is called erosion, and it forms caves which eventually wear through to arches. When the arches collapse, pillars of rock called stacks are left standing in the sea. Eventually, these crumble into the ocean, and the coastline is a little further back than it was before.

Direction of waves

Continental shelf

Around the edges of each continent, the ocean floor forms a wide shelf. The water there is shallow, warmer than the surrounding deep water and sunlit. It is full of ocean creatures. At the edge of the shelf, the ocean floor plunges steeply down to a cold, deep abyss where fewer animals survive.

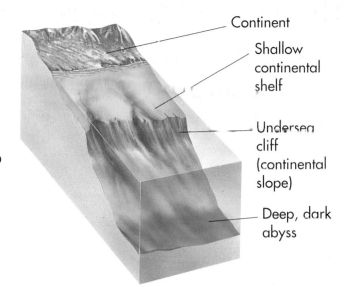

Continent

Shallow continental shelf

Undersea cliff (continental slope)

Deep, dark abyss

How coral reefs form

Many oceanic islands are the tips of underwater volcanoes. Coral reefs often grow around the edge, or fringe, of the islands where the water is warm and light (1).

The island begins to sink and wear away, more coral grows on top of existing coral to stay in the warmer, lighter surface waters and a barrier reef builds up. A broad stretch of sea, called a lagoon, separates the coral reef from the island (2).

The island continues to sink. When it disappears completely, a circular reef, or atoll, is left (3).

Coral reef

Coral reefs grow around tropical islands where the water is clean and warm. The tiny creatures that build them are very sensitive and will die if the water is too hot or too cold.

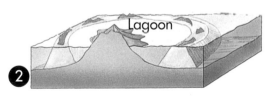

❶ Volcanic island Fringe reef

Lagoon

❷

Atoll

❸

TALKING POINT

Q: Many coral reefs around the world are dying! What do you think the reasons for this are?

A: Some reefs, like those off the coast of Florida, are being clogged by silt and poisoned by pollution. Others, like those around the Maldive Islands in the Indian Ocean, are dying because the sea temperature has risen and become too warm even for coral to survive.

Wind, waves and weather

The oceans are never still. The Sun's power drives the winds and makes the water move. Waves churn the surface and currents swirl round bays and surge across the seas, taking the weather with them. These patterns are also affected by the spinning of the Earth.

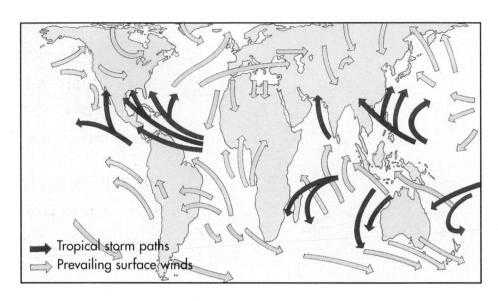

➡ Tropical storm paths
⇨ Prevailing surface winds

World wind patterns

The Sun's heat warms the air near the Equator and makes it rise. Cooler air rushes in from north and south to take its place, forming powerful winds. There are similar winds nearer the poles. The spinning of the Earth drags all the winds westwards.

World current patterns

Global ocean currents are closely linked to world wind patterns. Generally the currents move clockwise in the north and anticlockwise in the south. Cold currents flow from near the poles and warm currents flow from the Equator. There are also currents that flow vertically down to the depths and back to the surface.

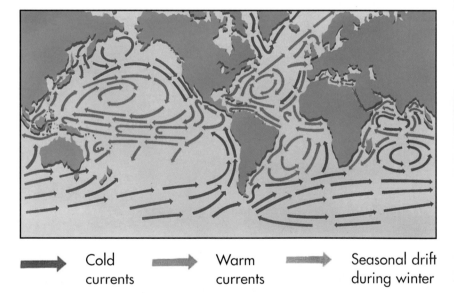

➡ Cold currents   ➡ Warm currents   ➡ Seasonal drift during winter

Hurricanes

Hurricanes are huge storms that usually form out at sea where cold winds meet warm winds. The air begins to swirl and a spinning column of storm clouds builds up (left). The storms can be over 650 km (400 miles) wide. The strong winds and heavy rain cause great damage if they reach land.

El Niño

Every few years, a warm current starts to flow the wrong way across the Pacific Ocean. It usually starts near Christmas time and is called El Niño, which means The Christ Child in Spanish. Scientists are still not sure why it happens. It causes catastrophic changes to the world's weather systems – cold, wet places have droughts and hot and dry places are flooded.

AUSTRALIA

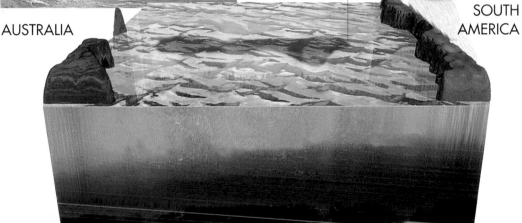

Warm water moves from Australia to South America.

Storm clouds form over South American deserts.

SOUTH AMERICA

Ocean conveyor belt

Cold water is heavier than warm water. So the cold water at the poles sinks. It flows along the seabed towards the Equator where it rises and warms up. It flows back towards the poles at the surface of the sea. This conveyor belt system is called the Polar Sink.

Freezing water squeezes out salt and sinks down.

Cold, deep water is carried back to the Equator.

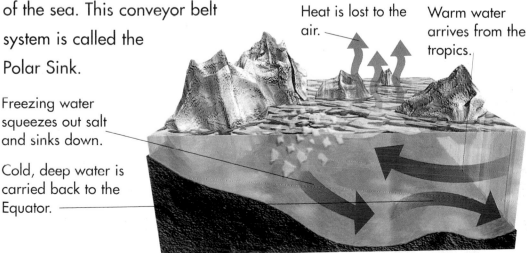

Heat is lost to the air.

Warm water arrives from the tropics.

Q: El Niño makes hot, dry places cool and wet, and it makes cool, wet places hot and dry. Is it good or bad?

A: It depends where you live. El Niño has caused devastation and billions of dollars worth of damage from drought and fires in many places. In a few places there have been unexpected bumper harvests. But extra rain is not always good. Somalia in Africa is a hot, dry country. In 1998, El Niño caused sudden rainstorms that led to terrible flooding and many crops were lost.

CHAPTER TWO

Life in the Oceans

The ocean ecosystem

The ocean is a giant ecosystem – plants and animals depend upon each other, and nothing is ever wasted. Like the land, the ocean gets its energy for life from the Sun. The energy is passed from plant to animal and from animal to animal in the form of food.

Rock pool world

Every rockpool is a miniature ecosystem. Winkles and limpets graze on the seaweed. Crabs and small fish chew on the shellfish and are in turn picked off by sea birds. Every time the tide comes in, it brings bits of food and refreshes the water.

The great white shark

The great white shark (below) is a high-speed killing machine with super senses. It is one of the ocean's top predators (hunters). Its favourite prey are seals and sea lions, but it will take a bite from anything it can catch. It can grow to more than six metres (18.5 feet) long, and has razor-sharp teeth.

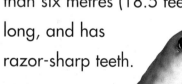

Creatures from the deep

Deep on the ocean floor, communities of giant worms, crabs and tiny fish live around hydrothermal vents – holes where super-hot water full of minerals gushes up from deep in the Earth's crust (above). Tiny bacteria feed on the minerals and provide food for the other creatures.

Food chains and webs

Minute floating plants, called plant plankton, form the basis of the ocean food chain. They are eaten by tiny surface animals that are, in turn, eaten by larger creatures. When they eventually die, they are eaten by detritus (waste) feeders on the seabed, such as sea cucumbers.

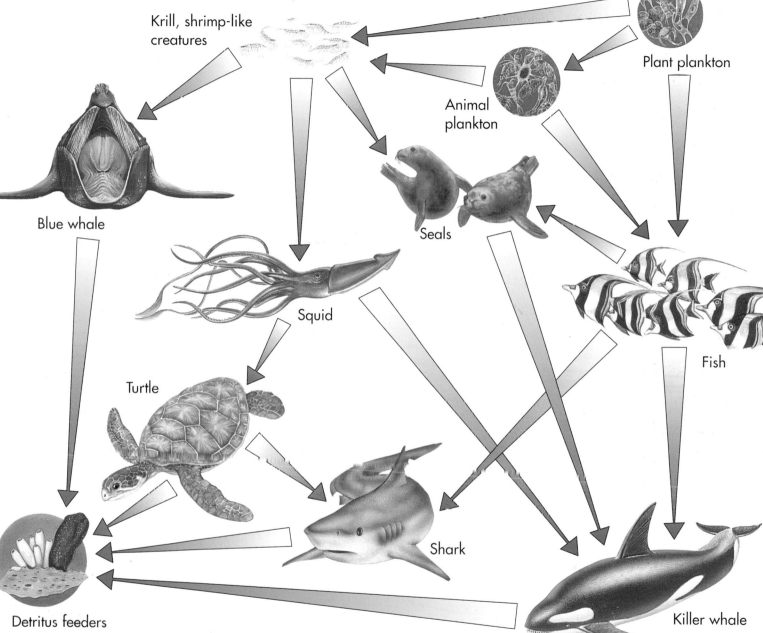

Sun

Plant plankton

Animal plankton

Krill, shrimp-like creatures

Blue whale

Seals

Squid

Turtle

Fish

Shark

Detritus feeders

Killer whale

TALKING POINT

Q: Sharks are among the ocean's top predators (hunters). Do they have any enemies?

A: Yes, they do. Big sharks, like great white sharks, have few enemies, but people kill 4.5 million sharks every year, for food, sport or just because they are in the way. All predators are important because they kill weak, sick and old animals. This helps to keep other species strong.

Relics and rainbows

Life began in the oceans and has been evolving there for thousands of millions of years. There are worms and wobbegongs, sea anemones and seahorses, crabs and clams – a wonderful variety of shapes, sizes and beautiful colours, each creature perfectly adapted to where it lives.

Coelacanth ▲

The coelacanth is a strange fish that is related to the ancestors of all land animals. Scientists thought it died out 65 million years ago like the dinosaurs. But now there are two known living colonies in the Indian Ocean.

Dark back scales

Light shade under the belly

▲ Counter-camouflage

Mackerel are pelagic – they swim near the surface of the open sea. Their belly-scales are silvery so they cannot be seen from below against the bright surface. Their back scales are darkly striped so they cannot be seen from above against the dark depths.

◄ Active disguise

Many bottom-living fish, like this plaice, can change the pattern on their bodies to match a sandy or a pebbly sea bed. They complete the disguise by flapping sand over the edges of their fins.

Deep-sea lights ▶

Food is hard to find in the dark depths of the ocean. So these weird-looking deep-sea fish lure victims with lights. They have huge teeth to make sure anything that comes near does not get away.

▼ Gentle giant

The whale shark is the biggest fish in the sea – it grows to over 13 m (40 ft) long. It is also one of the gentlest. To feed, it just opens its mouth and swims. It sieves tiny creatures from the water with its gills.

Deadly beauty ▲

The beautiful colours of the lion fish warn of danger. Each ray of its wafting fan-like fins is a hollow spine filled with lethal poison. Few other animals on the coral reef ever disturb this creature.

TALKING POINT

Q: Coelacanths have survived for 350 million years. But now they are dying out. Will they survive much longer?

A: The coelacanth population off the Comoros Islands near South Africa is sadly almost extinct. But recently a new species of coelacanth has been identified in the Indian Ocean around Indonesia. This population seems large and healthy.

Ocean people

The culture and history of coastal people are shaped by the ocean. The ocean provides their food, fuel, household utensils and ornaments to sell, and disposes of their refuse. Coastal people depend on boats for fishing and trade.

Island settlements

The huge Pacific Ocean is dotted with thousands of islands, both large and small. They were settled by ocean-going people from Southeast Asia thousands of years ago, using rafts and dugout canoes (above). These communities were totally dependent on their islands and the ocean for their survival.

Beach garbage

Almost every beach in the world has a tide-line of plastic rubbish that has been dumped out at sea and washed up by the waves. This rubbish can hurt and even kill sea animals if they eat it or get tangled in it. Metals and plastics last for many years in the sea.

Shipwreck

The ocean floor is littered with the wrecks of sunken ships. Some are hundreds of years old. Preserved by the cold salt water, some contain priceless treasures. Others contain valuable modern cargos. Recovering shipwrecks or the treasures they contain is called marine salvage. They can be a valuable source of income to archaeologists and historians.

Dugout canoe

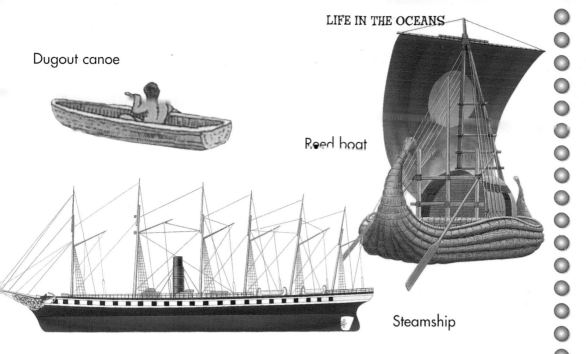

Reed boat

Steamship

History of boats

People have been using boats for five thousand years or more. The first were probably rafts and dugout canoes. These were probably pushed along with oars. Then the Egyptians discovered how to use sails to catch the wind. In the nineteenth century, ships were powered by steam engines but often still had sails.

Exploring the deep

Scientists have only recently been able to explore the depths of the ocean. Submersibles (right) can stand the huge deep-sea pressures without collapsing.

Sea gods

There are many mythical characters connected to the sea. Neptune (left) was the Roman god of the sea. He is still commemorated by celebrations on ships crossing the Equator.

TALKING POINT

Q: In days gone by, coastal people used the ocean as a rubbish tip. Can we go on throwing rubbish into the sea?

A: No. Small amounts of natural rubbish will rot away harmlessly in the sea. But now we dump 20 thousand million tonnes of rubbish in the sea every year. Much of it is plastic that will not rot away and may hurt or kill marine (sea) animals. There are also huge amounts of poisonous industrial chemicals dumped that can either kill or make marine plants and animals unhealthy, or make them poisonous to eat.

CHAPTER THREE

Ocean Bounty

Ocean treasures

The ocean has precious natural treasures to offer. There are valuable minerals in sea water and lying on the seabed. Oil and gas come from beneath the sea. Scientists are finding other ways of getting power from the sea.

Sea power

The picture (below) shows some of the many ingenious devices that have been invented to harness the energy in the sea to make electricity, using waves, tides and temperature differences. So far, few have proved successful.

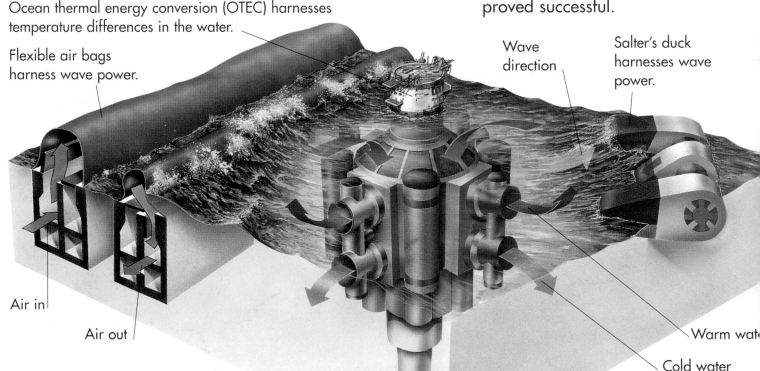

Ocean thermal energy conversion (OTEC) harnesses temperature differences in the water.

Flexible air bags harness wave power.

Wave direction

Salter's duck harnesses wave power.

Air in

Air out

Warm wat

Cold water

Fresh water from saltwater

This factory (right) is separating sea water into salt and fresh water (desalination). This is an expensive process, but it is used in some dry desert lands to irrigate the crops. With the ever-increasing need for fresh water, some people believe that desalting the ocean water is the answer to water shortages near sea coasts.

Precious boulders

Some parts of the deep ocean floor are strewn with lumps, or nodules, of pure manganese – a valuable mineral. But scraping it up by remote control (left) is still a very difficult and expensive procedure.

Wells in the ocean floor

Deep in the rocks beneath the ocean floor, there are pockets of oil and gas formed from the remains of tiny animals that died millions of years ago. At oil wells (below) holes are drilled down into the rocks, and the oil and gas are piped up to production platforms or to refineries on the shore.

Salt evaporation pans

Salt is a valuable mineral used in cooking and for making chemicals. Shallow pans are flooded with sea water. The Sun dries up all the water and leaves the salt crystals (below).

 **TALKING POINT**

The ocean is an unlimited and renewable energy source – that means it will never run out.

Q: Is this the answer to our future energy needs?

A: Not completely. At the moment, electricity from sea-driven power stations, such as tidal barrages or wave machines, is very expensive to produce and to deliver to nearby coastal homes and factories.

Ocean harvest

For centuries, fishermen and fisherwomen thought the sea's harvest of fish, shellfish and seaweed was inexhaustible. Today, most fish, over 90 million tonnes every year, are caught by giant factory ships with fleets of trawlers. So many fish have been caught that most of those that are left are too small to breed. Every day it is more difficult to find shoals of fish. Meanwhile many other animals are accidentally killed in the nets.

Herring

Herring

Herring are among the most important food-fish. About 4.5 million tonnes (5 million tons) are caught every year.

Mackerel

Mackerel live in large shoals in surface waters just offshore. They are caught in both the Atlantic and Pacific Oceans.

Mackerel

Seaweed

Seaweed

People have always collected seaweed for food. Today, it is grown in enclosures on land or in the sea and is used to make products such as jellies, cosmetics, medicines and diet foods.

Fishing methods

Individual fishermen and fisherwomen catch fish using rods, traps or small nets. Groups working on boats use large nets of different shapes and mesh-size (below) depending on the habits and size of the fish they want to catch.

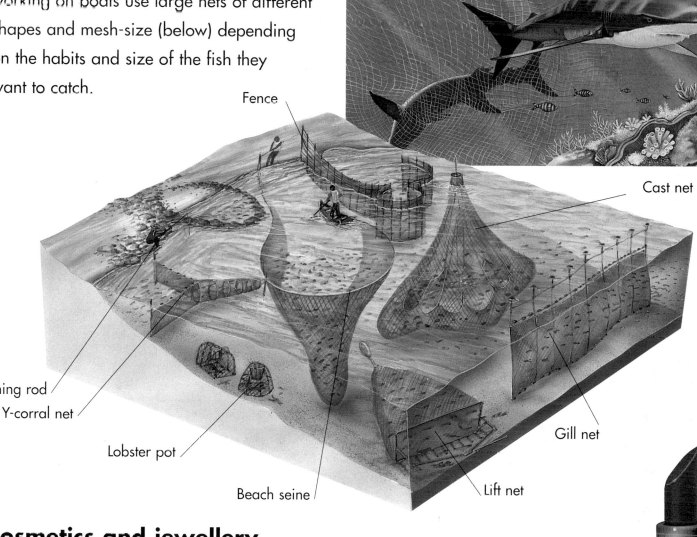

Fence

Cast net

Fishing rod

Y-corral net

Lobster pot

Beach seine

Lift net

Gill net

Cosmetics and jewellery

Food is not the only ocean harvest. Pearls are found inside oysters. Fish scraps are made into fertiliser. Fish not wanted for human consumption is turned into fishmeal and fed to farm animals. Fish oils, especially from sharks, are used to make cosmetics and face creams that are supposed to prevent wrinkles.

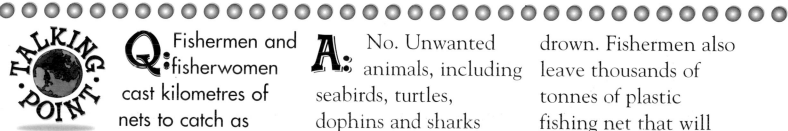

TALKING POINT

Q: Fishermen and fisherwomen cast kilometres of nets to catch as many fish as they can. Do they just catch fish for us to eat?

A: No. Unwanted animals, including seabirds, turtles, dophins and sharks (above), often get tangled in the nets and drown. Fishermen also leave thousands of tonnes of plastic fishing net that will never rot in the sea every year.

CHAPTER FOUR

Damaging the Oceans

Poisoning the oceans

The oceans are slowly turning into a poisonous soup, despite the huge volume of water. We are pouring in vast amounts of lethal chemicals, and these are killing or making the sea creatures sick, and damaging their young.

Pollution hotspots

The map shows where the worst pollution is happening. The hotspots are near the coasts where most people live. Waste pipes from factories and sewers empty untreated chemicals and sewage into the sea. Farm pesticides and fertilisers wash off the fields into rivers and into the sea. For example, the Mississippi River system carries pesticides and fertilisers to the Gulf of Mexico from two fifths of the United States' land surface. The North and Irish Seas are among the most radioactive in the world due to waste from nuclear reprocessing plants.

KEY

- very polluted
- polluted
- sometimes polluted
- may become polluted

Deadly spillage

Crude oil is thick, sticky and poisonous. If it leaks from the huge tanker ships that carry it, it floats on the surface of the sea and gets washed onto beaches. It clogs birds' feathers (left) so they cannot fly or swim. They swallow the oil, and they die.

◄ Toxic waste

Toxic means poisonous. For many years, factories have dumped their canisters of waste chemicals out at sea (left) hoping they will disappear in the depths. But the canisters begin to leak and the ocean currents bring the waste back up to poison the surface waters.

Ocean sewer ►

Sewage is what goes down the toilet! In many places in the world the sewers run straight into the sea. The sewage they carry is both unpleasant and dangerous. It contains germs that can cause illnesses, powerful cleaning chemicals that can poison and burn, and the end products of medicines that people have taken.

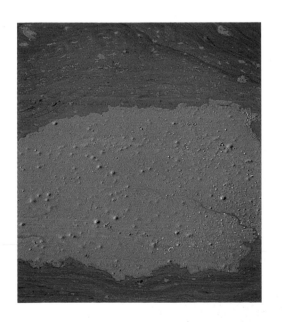

◄ Blooming algae

Algae are minute plants that float in the water. Normally they are a natural part of the ecosystem and are eaten by larger creatures. But when the water contains lots of sewage or fertilisers, the algae grow out of control and clog up the water, killing everything else.

TALKING POINT

Q: Oil tankers are massive ships that carry crude oil from oil wells out at sea to refineries on land. Can oil tankers kill animals?

A: Yes, they can. In March 1989, the oil tanker Exxon Valdez spilled 50,000 tonnes of oil along the coast of Alaska. The resulting oil slick covered 4,800 sq km (1,800 sq miles) of ocean and killed thousands of sea birds, sea otters, fish and shellfish. Even deer, bears and bald eagles on the nearby shore died.

Most endangered

The ocean contains untold numbers of animals and plants – it is the largest habitat (natural home) on Earth. We know very little about some of the animals, especially those that live in the depths. Many are in danger of becoming extinct and some will disappear even before they are discovered.

Green wanderer

Green turtles (above) may swim the oceans for 50 years before coming ashore to lay eggs. They are now very rare because they have been killed for their meat, shells and eggs, and their nesting beaches are covered with hotels and holiday-makers.

Coral reef

Coral reef communities are endangered. The sensitive coral animals are dying because of pollution, warming of the oceans and damage by some scuba divers. The colourful fish are caught for the tropical aquarium trade. Shellfish are caught for their lovely shells. Pretty coral is taken to be made into jewellery and sold to tourists.

Seals

Seals and sea lions have been killed for their fur and because fishermen think they eat too many fish or damage nets. Seals have also become diseased and died through pollution from the land (above).

Ocean giant

The blue whale is the largest animal ever to have lived on Earth, and, like most great whales, it almost became extinct because of whaling. Now most countries have stopped killing whales and their numbers are very slowly recovering.

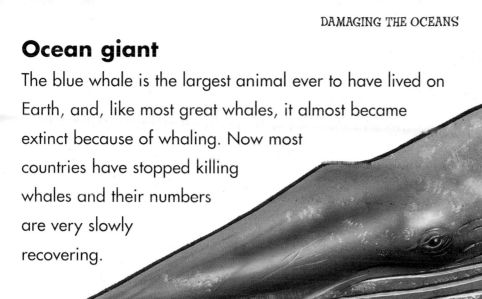

▼ Seahorses

Seahorses are small fish with heads like tiny horses. They live mostly in tropical waters. Their numbers are declining due to pollution and capture for the tourist trade and for use in Asian medicine.

Big tusker ▲

Walruses live in the Arctic Ocean. They have tusks like elephants. They use them for chipping ice, levering shellfish from rocks to eat, and for threatening rivals. Walruses are hunted for their meat, fatty blubber and ivory tusks. Hunting to sell the tusks has greatly reduced some populations.

TALKING POINT

Thousands of baby seals were once brutally clubbed to death every year for their soft, white fur.

Q: Do humans still kill seals?

A: Yes. Today, seals are culled (controlled numbers are killed) by shooting. This keeps their numbers down so that they do not take the fish that fishermen and fisherwomen want to catch.

CHAPTER FIVE

Solutions

Calling a halt

We cannot let the damage to the oceans continue. We have to stop the pollution and over-exploitation before it is too late. If we save the oceans, we will all benefit from the food, minerals and even medicines that they provide.

Whale watching

One way to help save ocean creatures is to let people see them. Whale-watching trips bring in money for conservation. They also educate people so they realise how precious and fragile the seas are. This kind of tourism is called eco-tourism to show it benefits the environment.

Treasures for sale

Many tourist centres sell starfish, coral, turtle shells, dead seahorses, and other bits of animals. These trinkets are far more beautiful when the animals are still alive in their natural home.

Dried starfish

Farming fish

Farming fish and shellfish in huge net enclosures (left) is one way of solving the fishing crisis. The pampered fish grow quickly and are easy to catch. But it has its disadvantages. Diseases and parasites spread quickly through the tightly packed shoals, so they are given medicines. Unfortunately, these drugs can kill other ocean creatures.

Great Barrier Reef

The Great Barrier Reef (below) is the largest and most spectacular reef on Earth. At more than 300,000 sq km (116,000 sq miles) it can be seen from outer space. It lies off the north-east coast of Australia and is a major attraction for tourists who come to see the variety of enchanting fish. It has been made into a World Heritage Site and a marine conservation park – the biggest in the world – to protect it from tourist damage and industrial pollution.

Trying to help

Many people and organisations, like Save the Whale, and Worldwide Fund for Nature, are campaigning to stop the destruction of the oceans. One of the most forceful is Greenpeace (right). Its members risk their lives by confronting the giant whaling ships and rubbish barges out at sea to try to stop their activities.

An enormous proportion of the world's whale population has been destroyed in the last hundred years by whaling fleets that killed whales for their meat and fat.

Q: Will whales die out?

A: Not yet. The Save the Whale campaign has led to an almost world-wide ban on whaling. The great whales are gradually recovering. Only two countries, Japan and Norway, still hunt great whales. Some other creatures like monk seals and green turtles may not be so lucky.

Look Back and Find

Now it is time for you to test your knowledge. On these two pages are many questions about the topics covered in this book. First of all, look at the pictures. What can you remember about them?

Water world

How many oceans are there?
What are their names?
How much of the Earth's surface is covered in water?
How deep are the oceans?
Where did the water for the oceans come from?
How does water go round in a cycle?

Around the edges

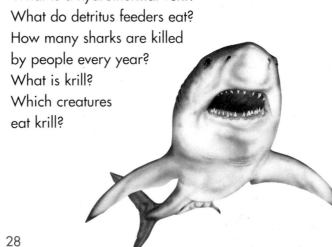

Are there mountains under the sea?
Where does the ocean floor form?
How does the ocean floor form?
Name some features you can see on the coast.
Where does coral live?
Why are the coral reefs in Florida and the Maldives dying?

Stormy seas

What is El Niño and where does it happen?
What happens to cold water at the North Pole?
What happens to warm water at the Equator?
What does the spinning of the Earth do to the wind?
What is a hurricane?

Food chains

What do great white sharks like to eat best?
What is a hydrothermal vent?
What do detritus feeders eat?
How many sharks are killed by people every year?
What is krill?
Which creatures eat krill?

Every size, shape and colour

Why are mackerel coloured dark on top and light underneath?
When did scientists think the coelacanth had died out?
Which fish can change the pattern on its body to match its surroundings?
What does the largest shark in the sea eat?
Which fish produce their own light?
Why are some deadly fish brightly coloured?

People and the ocean

What kind of rubbish can you find on the beach?

Why is it there?

What was an early type of boat?

How did the first people get across the Pacific Ocean?

Who discovered how to use a sail first?

What do scientists use to explore the deep ocean?

Water and salt

Name one way of making electricity from seawater.

What is desalination? Where is desalination most used?

How is salt taken out of seawater?

Which mineral lies as boulders on the ocean floor?

Where does oil come from?

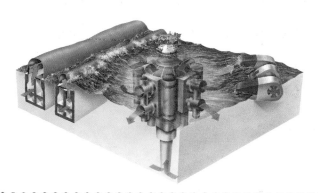

Fish and nets

How much fish do fishermen catch every year?

Have we taken too many fish out of the sea?

What do we use seaweed for?

Name some types of nets used by fishermen.

What kinds of animals get caught in these nets?

Ocean poison

Name some places in the world where ocean pollution is very bad (remember the map).

What do we put into the sea to make it dirty and dangerous?

What happens to algae in pollution? Is this bad for fish? What happened off the coast of Alaska in 1989?

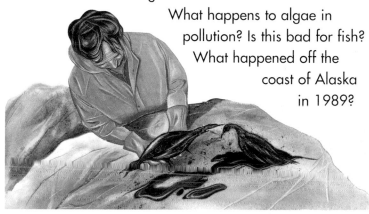

Animals in danger

Name some animals in danger of extinction. How long may a green turtle live before it even begins to breed?

Why do people collect and dry out starfish?

Why do people kill walruses?

Are whales in danger of extinction?

Stopping the damage

What is whale watching?

Why do people do it?

Why do people farm fish? Where are the fish kept? Name one disadvantage to fish farming.

Name an organisation that tries to protect the oceans and the animals in them.

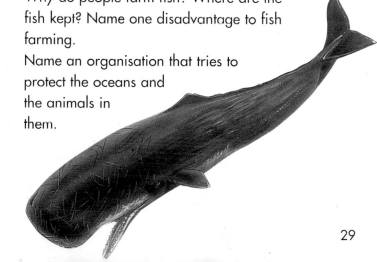

You Be Environmental!

The oceans are enormous – they seem too big for us to hurt them. But we are polluting them, taking too many fish, and harming countless sea animals. There are things that you can do to help save the oceans. You can write to your member of parliament to show your concern. Don't buy things made at the expense of the ocean animals, such as coral necklaces.

Energy-saving houses cut down on electricity use, reducing the need for oil wells in the oceans. This in turn reduces ocean pollution.

Recycling helps the environment, including the oceans, which could otherwise fill up with dumped rubbish.

Use water carefully. This reduces the amounts passed as waste into the sea.

Vehicle exhausts and all kinds of fires pollute the atmosphere. This may worsen global warming and affect the ocean's currents, plants and animals.

Design your own environmental poster!

Here are some useful addresses for you to get more information.

Friends of the Earth
26-28 Underwood Street,
London N1 7JQ

Greenpeace
Canonbury Villas,
London N1 2PN

Worldwide Fund for Nature
Panda House,
Weyside Park,
Cattleshall Lane,
Godalming,
Surrey
GU7 1XR

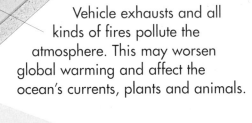

GLOSSARY

Atmosphere
The air; the layers of gases that surround the surface of the Earth.

Bacteria
Very tiny living things that are too small to see with the naked eye. The harmful ones are sometimes called germs.

Carbon dioxide
One of the gases that makes up the air; it is one of the "greenhouse gases" that are causing global warming.

Condensation
When a gas or vapour turns into a liquid; for example, when steam turns into water.

Crude oil
The thick, raw oil (petroleum) that comes up from deep in the Earth. It is turned into petrol or used in many industries.

Crust
The outer solid, rocky layer of the Earth.

Culling
Controlled, humane killing of animals to prevent them from becoming too numerous.

Desalination
Removing salt from sea water to produce pure water for drinking or for watering plants, such as crops.

Evaporation
When a liquid turns into a gas or vapour; for example, when wet washing dries, the water turns into water

vapour in the air.

Exploitation
Using the Earth's resources for the benefit of people but not for the benefit of the Earth.

Extinction
When all the animals or plants of one kind (species) have died out.

Fertilisers
Natural substances or chemicals that farmers use to make their crops grow better.

Pollution
All the poisons and rubbish in the air, soil and water which are harming animals and plants and making people ill.

Radioactive
Substances that give out dangerous invisible rays that can cause illness or death.

Renewable power
Electricity made from energy sources that will never run out such as the Sun, the wind or the waves.

Sodium chloride
Salt, a chemical made of sodium and chlorine, found in sea water.

Subduction zone
Where the oceanic crust sinks beneath the continental crust.

Submersible
An underwater craft that can dive down to very deep water.

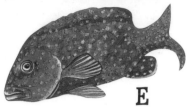

INDEX

Picture Credits

Abbreviations: t-top, m-middle, b-bottom, r-right, l-left, c-centre.
Cover - Roger Vlitos. 4, 5, 9, 10, 11, 16 both, 18, 19, 24, 26 bl & 27 - Frank Spooner Pictures.
23m - Bruce Coleman Collection. 23b & 26 br - Oxford Scientific Films.